MW01673282

One More Before I Leave

by Nonya Charmel

DORRANCE
PUBLISHING CO
EST. 1920
PITTSBURGH, PENNSYLVANIA 15238

Dorrance Publishing Co
585 Alpha Drive
Pittsburgh, PA 15238
Visit our website at *www.dorrancebookstore.com*

ISBN: 978-1-6366-1280-5
eISBN: 978-1-6366-1866-1

One More Before I Leave

Introduction

The thirst for writing was reestablished when I enrolled in a memoir writing class. I remember thinking who would be interested in my life, or what can I share without anyone getting upset with me. Needless to say, that was the breakthrough I needed to finally come to terms with tragedies, love, betrayal, alienation, and just living life.

My collection of writings are my memoirs based on true events. It worked as a therapeutic exercise leading to my inner healing to take place. Doing this allowed me to finally be at peace with myself. Because of the boost of confidence along with encouraging words from my memoir instructor, Carlene Blake-Hudson, PHD, I was able to accomplish my dream of writing again.

Did I Tell You

There is nothing quite like the evening breeze in early September. The cool air blowing right through my body, touching every inch of my inner core, and relaxing my mind at the same time. As I take in a deep breath, the relaxing sensation massages my being in a soothing, seducing, and forbidding way. The perfect combination for achieving the ultimate climax in the company of one.

When I first met you, I was immediately attracted to you. Your dazzling smile that showcased bleached white, perfectly aligned teeth, with a debonair smile. My heart was assigned to you forever. It was at that precise moment I knew my life could not continue without you in it. The most encouraging part was that your heart was connected to mine from the start. The love that radiated between us intoxicated everyone who came in our presence.

Life always seemed to continuously move in a positive direction with you around. Life just simply made sense. To be in sync would properly describe our relationship. We became our own personal psychics, the ability to read each other's minds intensified whenever we bonded our souls as one. The synergy that ignited, set the atmosphere on fire, soaring us to unbridled ecstasy beyond this natural world. I could nor would ever love anyone else but you.

Being on a high note can make you blind to reality. Was it that I assumed you were happy with me? Did you think I abandoned you when you needed me the most? I expressed my disappointments only to better improve our relationship; it was never intended to break you to the point of no return. I sensed it when you looked into my eyes, which were vacant. No longer did you have that sparkle of happiness shining through those beautiful, chestnut brown eyes. When I asked to have your final forgiveness, I would have never imagined in a million years you would take that last step and close me out forever. My heart died when you said goodbye.

Did I tell you how much you completed me? Did I tell you that you alone repaired my esteem? You encouraged me to dream, step out to act on what I wanted, and never settle for anything less than perfect. Did I tell you how your hugs warmed me right down to the bones? I felt secured, protected, loved, and nurtured in your loving arms. Did I tell you how soothing your heartbeat was when I was pressed against your massive godlike arms? The beats in perfect rhythm with each breath you inhaled and exhaled drawing me in closer and never letting go.

I struggle with the fact I had the opportunity to tell you all of those things before your demise. Just because it was sudden, doesn't excuse my delay in telling you all of the great things I had in you. Perhaps this eulogy I am giving in remembrance of you can bring me closure. Maybe my words will be carried to Heaven straight to your ears to allow you to have real, eternal peace. That is all I can hope for now and attempt to go on with living life without you.

The funniest thing happened exactly one year after I said my final goodbye to you. A cool breeze penetrated me on this early September evening. It was different this time because I felt your arms around me holding me tight. You whispered as the wind took you away, "I love you forever, and I forgive you."

Forgiveness

Today, I have chosen to take my power back and finally heal from the damage you left behind. For years, I viewed myself through the scope of your eyes. To see through your eyes, NO ONE was ever good enough, smart enough, beautiful enough, or cultured enough. In your eyes, you only accepted those who were sophisticated, well learned, and monetarily sustained. You would rule with fear and control simply with venomous words. This would result in generations seeking approval in all forms imaginable, proving that the power of negative WORDS COULD AND WOULD HARM. Having an ending result of absolutely no self-value but secretly self-loathing and hating of one's self.

I remember the exact words you used this time that finally beat me down. In my eyes, I saw my appearance as beautiful this particular day. I just had my hair braided like Janet Jackson's character in the movie *Poetic Justice*. I walked home that hot summer evening, glowing with self-esteem, partly due to all of the compliments from the neighborhood people. I came inside of the house and stood at the door smiling because I was proud. Everyone looked and said, "Wow you look so beautiful! What a wonderful job she did on your hair."

Before I could answer, I watched you push your way through with a scowling expression. Everyone present stopped talking and silence filled the room, anxiously anticipating the venomous words that followed.

Our eyes connected and at that point you gained power over my soul. You shook your head in utter disgust and said, "YOU LOOK UGLY!"

I felt such excruciating pain tear through my heart, down my rib-cage, and to the pit of my stomach. It was like you took a sword, plunged it into me slowly, sliced down, and disemboweled me. My emotions immediately were triggered to start crying, however, due to my defense mechanism developed over the years, it overpowered and made me emotionless. I guess I could thank you for this "ability."

In the fog I heard yelling from those present in the room. One person yelled, "Why would you say something like that? Why do you always do this?"

Another person would say to me, "Don't listen to her, you look beautiful."

They tried to comfort me but the damage was done. The words you used to disembowel me finally took its toll.

In my late thirties, I learned to love myself. After I received spiritual counseling, I gained the confidence I needed to uproot your bitter words from my heart. I had to forgive you in order to move on with my life.

Well, I forgive you and release you from my soul. I choose to view you as a person who was damaged and only knew how to inflict damage on others. I could never term the title "grandmother," since you made it clear numerous times I was not welcomed. It was a vivid contrast compared to my maternal grandma, who loved me unconditional. I take comfort believing that you were not a cold-hearted and hate-filled person, which was the way I knew you, but that you only repeated what was done to you in life growing up.

The Forgotten One

Do you ever think about me? It seems like it was so long ago, the last time we conversed, when I asked how you felt. Please! DON'T YOU EVER think you're forgotten about, or that I erased your total existence from my memory! But, I must confess, I did bury you deeply into my subconscious. I knew this would be the only way I could function through this mortal life without you. The truth is, I'm a coward, I'm weak, and I'm selfish, with ice flowing through my veins. At least that's how I viewed myself and the actions I took that afternoon, which made you vanish from our world for good.

It was an attempt to give you the best life you could ever imagine. The torment and self-hatred that flowed through out my soul as I felt every part of you. Each day ripening as one being inside of me. Every movement you made, every breath you breathed, every turn you took, and stretch and kick you took to make me aware of your presence. Feeling it to my very core as I sank further into loneliness and heart break unrepairable. I tried to be positive; please believe that, but the more I tried, the darkness was more powerful and consumed me further into the corner. I had rather have us both leave this pain, not just you go alone.

Did you feel the pain when the stranger disrupted your calm, warm, safe, and secure resting place? Was it a gentle transition? Oh, God, I hope it was! I don't think my heart could take it if you said you felt the instruments hook you. Without any compassion or sympathy, did they look at you as trash and toss you away, only keeping parts they felt was of value and nothing more? I know you ask from your perfect place of rest, "Mom, why wasn't I allowed to be developed and nourished to live out a wonderful life?"

I could only answer you with two simple, but powerful words: I'M SORRY.

I never gave you a name, I guess because I didn't know what gender would be the most dominant if you had the opportunity to have gotten that far. You never did in this reality, but in my pretend perfect world for you, you did. You see, I imagine this storyline for you, which took place after your abrupt departure from my womb. In this perfect world, you had people around you to love you and provide everything you could want and need unconditional, something I could not have wholly done, and I could only have given you the unconditional love part.

I saw you smiling at me as you ran into my arms. The smell of fresh cut lavender lilacs poured out of your very essences. We sat down in the greenest of grass, with the clearest bluest of blue skies, and huge marshmallow clouds that were so close we could bite them. You told me about your amazing life journey's that seemed to be almost impossible to believe. Then I was able to view it through the portal of time you had the power to open. You kissed my cheek and said how much you have and always will love me, then you slowly disappeared as you stepped through the portal you possessed the power to have.

I just yelled, "I LOVE YOU, AND I'M SORRY!"

You appeared in the blink of an eye and said, "Mom, I forgive you, and love you too!"

That would be the last time I would ever see you.

The truth hurts entirely too much, and always ends with me holding on with my fingertips. Allowing me to slip further into that dark infinity black hole, never to be seen again. It seems better to give a happy life, even if it is a pretend happy one, just to be able to conquer this life until I can join you.

Shattered

The earth-shattering event that took place on that late afternoon on May 12, 1990, changed my life forever. I was never able to properly heal, grieve, be happy, live, or discuss what happened that day with anyone. Although I was not alone when it happened, you leaving us stopped the hands of time in all of our lives. You left us stuck in the tragedy that would remain a taboo subject for years to come.

Can I ask you a question, Grandma? Why did it take you so long to reach out for help? Was it because you were just as shocked as we all were when it snuck up on you? Did you stay quiet not to cause a scene since it was the day before Mother's Day? I hope it was not for my sake that you would endure pain for my happiness. I regret not being older, more alert to your needs, and bolder, so I could have held your hand and comforted you before you left. I think I hate myself the most for that, not being there for you like you had always been there for me.

I decided to write down all the events of that infamous day because I'm not emotionally strong enough to speak it out loud. To acknowledge what had taken place meant it really did happen, and forced me to have felt emotions I had locked up in a vault. Perhaps

I can write this memoir to you, Grandma. I believe it will help me heal and let you rest in peace finally after 30 years.

At 13-and-a-half years old, I was consumed with my own issues. I was watching television with my sister and thinking, "Why is Grandma not out here with us?" I heard scrabbling from the back coming towards the front of the apartment; it was my mom running, and then grabbing the house phone. I watched this sitting on the couch, clueless as to why complete panic was on her face. She proceeded to use the phone, and since the cord was long it stretched from the kitchen to the back. She used a hand gesture directing me to go in the back where Grandma was.

With my eyes fixated on Grandma, I watched in horror as she clutched her chest, tried to catch her breath, and forced a smile for me. She had mustered up enough of her breath to say, "I am okay."

As I looked up in her loving eyes that were filled with embarrassment, tears, sadness, pain, and fear, she closed the bathroom. I just stood there saying, "Grandma, are you okay? Grandma, are you okay?"

She never responded back to me and then my mom yelled, "Why are you not watching her! I told you to watch her, Nonya!"

I said, "I was, but she closed the door, Mommy!"

All I heard was the address being repeated over the phone. Suddenly, I could hear a lot of voices in the apartment, but none familiar to me. It sounded like banging and furniture being moved around. At this point, I stayed in Grandma's bedroom, where it was safe. I caught a glimpse of a fireman as my mom closed the door of the bedroom. I assumed she felt it would shield me from seeing anything that would further traumatize me.

It was the next day, Mother's day, and my mom and great aunt (my grandma's closest sister) wanted to tell the news to the guests in person instead of over the phone. Aunt "fragile" came in all smiles with her granddaughter, who was my cousin. Before telling her the bomb dropping news, I was asked to take my sister and cousin into grandma's bedroom and close the door. I did, but this time, I stayed in the back hallway hidden. I heard the news about why Grandma was not back home to celebrate Mother's Day.

What I heard, or what I could mentally process was that grandma was having a heart attack when she forced a smile at me and closed the door. She had passed away in the ambulance, but the EMTs revived her as my mom and great aunt rode in the back with her. She became comatose and remained in that state for the next five months before passing away. Adults believe that keeping secrets, whispering, and leaving children out of conversations is the best way to protect them. That can actually have the opposite effect, unfortunately.

After that, life just seemed to move around me as I stood frozen. I went through the motions like everyone else, pretending life had moved on, but holidays stopped being celebrated completely. I never really processed everything that had happened, only internalized it completely. No one talked about what had happened on that Saturday, the day before Mother's Day; it was almost taboo to bring it up. It was not until I had my daughter five years later that I found out her birthday was the day before grandma passed away. It was an awkward silence after that statement. As usual another subject was quickly discussed to break the uncomfortable feeling in the air. Expressed emotions never were a welcomed visitor, only if in private and alone, but never encouraged to be seen.

My happy memories were with Grandma being the center of it. Everything we did was at her house, including holiday celebrations. I just remember the emptiness I felt when my life was shattered that day before Mother's Day. I grew to hate that Saturday before Mother's Day. I always had to tip toe around until that holiday passed, then go back to the "new normal" until the next dreaded holiday.

Well, Grandma, I think I am able to live my life now. I thank you for listening to me express my pain to you. I held on to you, not allowing you to rest in peace, I am so sorry for that. Writing this to you helped me grieve the loss of you, and now, I can let you go. I love you with all of my heart and look forward to seeing you again.

One More Before I Leave

Should I finally go on and admit that your power of seduction is impossible to quit? But if I do, that means you win. I must find a way to refuse the constant temptation to indulge in your harmful delights. Please don't look at me that way; I can't do this anymore!

This is insane to think after all of these years, the outcome can be different. A vicious cycle of broken promises left questioning my self-worth. I HATE HOW I ACT when I allow you to enter me! The first taste of you on my tongue, bitter and then burning my throat as I swallow you down in one gulp. Obviously this is the clear indication of how hazardous you can truly be. But I ignore it, and take in more of you until we are one. You having full control of my thoughts, body, and actions. Having me relinquish all my will to your total control. Is there something wrong with me because I love the power and confidence I feel when you are in control? Or have I just accepted the unhealthy relationship we have as normal?

Is this how it will always end when you're done with me? With me feeling the plush carpeting in between my fingers as I try to figure out where I am. Not being able to remember how I ended up lying flat on the floor on my stomach, half-way dressed. Now having to get up slowly in excruciating pain, crawl to the bed with my head pounding, and throat feeling like sand paper hurting each time I try to swallow. As I lay down under the covers with fresh bruises on my arms, legs, and the bottom of my chin, I try to remember what happened. But I can't remember anything of last night events because as usual you wipe out any memory of what WE do.

In bits and pieces, it always comes back, such as conversing with people during that night and seeing confusion in their expressions. Leaving me to wonder what did I say and how did I act. It's so embarrassing when everyone can remember your behavior except you. I just hate myself for allowing you to do this yet again to me. Enough is enough. The decision has been made to quit you for good. Whisky, I will never partake in drinking you again, we are done!

Jack

Jack introduced me to a world that was beyond my reach. I thought it was something I could survive but was sadly mistaken. Jack devoured my innocence and destroyed my soul.

Jack was a very smooth gentleman with a deep caramel color. He had an intoxicating smell that lingered when he left any room he entered. When he kissed you, WOW! I still to this day do not know how his taste stayed on my tongue for days. Jack hooked you the minute you tasted him!

Jack's demeanor was seductive with the hint of a serial killer bite to him. The charming way he introduced himself was unforgettable. Jack always insisted on giving eye contact; this way he could extract your soul. He overpowered anyone who put up a fight because he was, and still is, a master craftsman in everything he touches.

This night was like every night with one exception, Jack's serial killer side was not under control. I had absolutely no clue that this would be the last time I would ever see Jack. He started out with his usual smooth consistency, and I began to suddenly feel a simmering fire move up from my stomach towards the middle of my chest. My legs began to buckle underneath me as I tried to talk. Shortly after that, my speech was incoherent, and my vision faded into black.

Although my whole body was incapacitated, I could hear everything in my surroundings. Jack's voice was the loudest and most distinct yelli,ng, "Look how seductive you are being, licking your lips and asking for something to put in your mouth. Wow! Look how much of a pro you are stripping off your clothes for all the men in here. This must be your side job because your dancing is better than the professionals who get paid to do this. OMG! Why are you performing on those guys? You are the nastiest whore I have ever met in my life! Go to hell!"

I slowly gained my sight back and the mobility of my body functions. It seemed like it was a lifetime that passed by, but in fact it was only 30 minutes. I smelled the mixture of Jack's intoxicating aroma with freshly dried vomit. My head felt like a hammer was lodged into my scalp and hemorrhaging out blood. I noticed everyone was standing on the side of the room in shock as I held on to the walls to stand myself up. I looked for Jack, but he was no place to be found.

My throat felt like sandpaper each time I attempted to swallow without any saliva. I managed with every ounce of strength in my body to yell out, "Jack! Where are you? I need your help. Please come and get me and take me home now!"

A woman came and assisted me to the table where a chair was at. She seemed to be so puzzled at what I had just yelled. I asked her if she saw Jack. I described him to her, but with no avail; she had no clue as to whom I was talking about. Tears of frustration rolled down my face because Jack left me all alone.

I just sat there staring straight in disbelief until I heard a voice in the background. It was faint, but I can still hear it over the chatter in the room.

A hand touched me lightly on my shoulder, and the woman leaned in to whisper something in my ear. I turned and looked in her face, and she said, "Miss, are you still looking for Jack?"

I said with total excitement, "YES! I am! Do you know him? Where did he go?"

She handed me a bottle of whiskey with the words "Jack" written across it. I looked and said, "Thanks, sweetie, but Jack is a person not a drink." I explained I was with him the whole night, and he was yelling over everyone there.

Silence filled the room followed by gasps. I was confused by the reaction of everyone in the room. I asked, "Why is everyone acting weird? Did I miss something? Where is Jack?"

The woman kneeled down in front of me, took my hand, and looked in my eyes with compassion. She explained to me that I came in alone and was at the bar with the bottle of "Jack" drinking alone. I began to take of my clothes for everyone as they looked on in horror. It was also specified that the medics was about to be called if I hadn't woken up in the next five minutes. She mentioned I just kept talking to the whiskey bottle of "Jack" for the whole night and no one else.

As I gathered the information being told to me, bits and pieces of the night started to come back. The serial killer Jack was actually in my own head, not a real person. It was, in fact, me who was the one with a hint of serial killer inside. But when I incorporated whisky with my inner personality, I took on the form of Jack.

My Song of Solomon

The sensation of pure unbashful delights ponders in my mind with every step you take towards me. My mouth salivates like a dog about to steal that juicy delicious chop sitting on the edge of the table. The aromas of sweat, musk, cologne, and body secretions permeate the air. Don't you know I can smell you from miles away? I can even smell your blood as it flows through every vein in your body. Our supernatural connection allows us to become conjoined as one to explore total ecstasy.

The enjoyment as I feel the light touch of your fingers glide gently over my being is amazing. Your lips soft and partially opened, so I can feel your breath blow and tease me. The tips of your fingers massaging my erect special areas causing my fluids to drip. As I squirm from the overflow of excitement, I feel the palm of your hand hold me down in loving fashion. Your hands sculptured by the gods themselves, because only they can craft a sexual masterpiece like that. Each of your fingers measuring the size of a normal persons two fingers, with the perfectly rounded, blunted shaped thumb to finish off its beauty.

As you rub your finger from the gods along my lips, I can feel your heart racing with expectation. Your pupils dilate, enhancing the deep blue color in your eyes. You look deep into my eyes, fixated on my every facial expression as it feeds your appetite. You come in closer, placing your lips above mine but too far to feel. First, your tongue starts out to taste my lips, following the invitation into my mouth. The taste of sweet nectar lingered on your tongue from licking my other lips. A taste so addictive it sealed us together as one.

Standing in full view of the glass-stained windows, your skin glistening from the sun, showing the beads of sweat on your body. The eggshell, milky-white complexion, with red chest hair covering your perfect pecks in a circular design. Your body mirroring Zeus, but the face of Adonis with light freckles as a decoration from the gods. My will and being totally submitted to you forever.

I begin to explore as if reading braille, using my fingertips as a guide to understanding your body. I massage the top of your head, slowly rubbing your velvet hair. I lean in, rub my face on the left side of your head lightly kissing your ear. As you rest your head on my extra fluffy, natural pillows, you allow me to kiss the top of your head. We just hold each other elongating this moment in time. You lift your head, piercing my soul with your steel blue eyes, saying, "I love you to the core."

Now, I lean into you, taking in your tongue and breath, in a rhythmic movement as one soul. I can feel your heartbeat racing as I massage down your back. You wrap your massive arms around my waist, thrusting me into you. I can feel your excitement as you press towards me. I lose control of my thoughts, so I can allow every throbbing sensation to be fully pleasured. I feel your hand press perfectly around my neck, sending me into a whirlwind of absolute pleasure. I slowly disconnect into the level of pure unadulterated sexual bliss.

I take in your ravenous appetite as I stretch with every deepening stroke. Every nerve in my inner core heightening and receiving the godlike girth, transporting me to the realm of unfiltered delights.

I hear my soul moaning and begging to be released, but I deny it. It only can be allowed to peak when it's at its fullness. You unleash all of your creaminess through me, penetrating all of my soul, and allowing me to peak and release at its fullness. Everything becomes motionless and calm, just the light breeze from the stain glass windows moved in the room.

Silenced Voice

Can you hear my voice in the midst of chaos? Are my feelings put on display or simply erased like an afterthought? Why are my concerns, fears, inequalities, and vulnerabilities trashed and torn to pieces? Does my life matter to anyone? Why am I viewed lesser than human and not protected? My words are constantly ridiculed, scrutinized, and defamed by those it is expressed to.

My cry is silenced, my pain is dismissed, and my worth is devalued and turned into public shaming. Why do you mistreat me, belittle me, abuse me, sexualize me, discard me, and abandon me? Am I not worth anything to you? My tears that roll down my face from constant frustration has FORCED me to be STRONG, SELF-RELIANT, BITTER, ENYOUS, HATFUL, POWERFUL, BROKEN, LONELY, SELF-LOATHING, AND DESTRUCTIVE.

Why is there no outrage when my virtue is stolen? I guess because my skin color is not viewed as being part of an elite race. The constant reminder engraved in society of how much "better" my female white counterpart is. My features and skin tone discussed in a public forum as a contagious disease in desperate need to be cleansed. Why am I so UGLY to you? My hair texture if not seen as "good hair" is an abomination to some of my black male counterparts. Is it such a curse for a successful black male to have a black woman? Unfortunately, the constant berating is used as a platform for most black athletes. A public spectacle as they parade white women as being the pinnacle of truly accomplishing success. But if I go out of the "race pool," I am verbally, psychologically, and physically attacked by some of the very men who hold every other women who is not black in the highest regard.

Society is fixated on black women being symbols of sexual pleasures but not of any worth. When a black female child, teen, or adult is missing, there is no search party with every news outlet doing there due diligence in finding her. Animals will get more attention when being mistreated than a black woman.

Why is it when a black woman complains, the words and thoughts that usually follow are, "So what did you do to cause this to happen to you? You probably provoked him/her to do this to you. I bet you asked for it and now pretending you have changed your mind." The feeling of protection is null and voided. Trust, well, to say the least, is non-existent.

A black woman is hated on, molested on, defiled on, brutalized on, diminished on, ostracized, and slowly being obviated. In order to survive this genocide, WE as black women must love and treasure our own worth and value. Is it a huge disappointment when WE are not praised for just simply being present? Absolutely it is, but to give in to it will lead to our end. I have elected to be a strong, confident, proud black woman who my God took meticulous time to create. When I decide to focus on that, NO man, women, boy, or girl can strip me of this confidence. Therefore, I will use whatever tools I have available to me, so I can encourage all the black women. Especially those out there feeling forgotten and worthless. If one word is read that can change the mindset and heart of a black women, then my job has been accomplished.

To the black women who read this: know you are beautiful, wonderful, a priceless treasure, and uniquely created by God, Stay encouraged always, from one black women to many others.

The Battle Within

At the tender age of seven, I was developed in a voluminous way and slightly meaty. I was the only one in my class who had to wear a bra. Like every child, you don't realize that you are different until someone tells you. I was able to keep up with everyone in sports, I climbed the monkey bars, did relay races, jumped rope, played hand ball, did handstands and even cartwheels. I realized I was not like every other little girl when I had my first crush. Having the innocence of a child, I freely expressed my feelings to my friends. I even wrote a note in class saying, "Do you like me? Please check yes or no." When the note made it back to me on the other side of the class, I opened it and saw the crushing word "NO"!

It was the last days before graduating from the sixth grade in June. I remember being so happy and enjoying making memories with my friends I would never see again. We all took pride in folding each pastel colored page in our autograph books. I have no clue as to why we would fold the pages; we just knew it was the proper thing to do. It was EXTREMELY important that everyone had a note and signature from each person in the class, even if you were not friends. It was the amount of signatures that counted that made you feel important. Proper protocol was not to read what people wrote until the end of the school day.

As I peered through my book at home, I remember the most common thing that was written, it was, "Hey stay sweet and nice! Take care and enjoy junior high school." It was only one note that stung me to the core. It was from "the Casanova" of the class, who was the only boy at that age with a bottle of cologne in his desk. At every given moment, he would spray his neck, pop his collar up on his shirt, and smile at everyone in the class. He was one of a kind and nice to everyone. What he wrote wasn't intended in a malicious way; however, words have a lasting effect regardless.

As I unfolded the paper to read the next friendly note, it was from him. This is what his note said to me, "Too Pretty, and Fat, to be forgotten." I smiled at the pretty part, but as I read "fat," it crushed me, and I cried. Life, being the cruel mistress that she is, taught me early about self-image and acceptance. I learned to process my self-esteem through the eyes of others, leading to unhealthy life choices. I accepted that I was not a tantalizing treat to others, so I accepted what was given to me. How can I expect to be treated in a loving fashion when I didn't think I was deserving of it?

In junior high school, the mocking continued in my gym class. I was in eighth grade and in our school eighth grade was numbered from the smartest to the not too smart. The "AP" was the smartest and then it was 8-1, 8-2, and last 8-8. Well out of those classes each gym had four eighth grade classes combined. At the end of the semester, it was an obstacle course that had to be completed in order to pass gym. It was something that was practiced in groups each gym session, with everyone sitting along the walls to watch your performance. I never understood the concept of this, why on Earth would it be perceived that students would do a great job as their peers laughed, mocked, and/or cheered for them? This very practice left a lasting effect on me to adulthood. So each time I had to run, I placed my left forearm over my breasts to hold them down from bouncing up and down as I ran. It was one boy that would make it his mission in life to laugh and run around mocking how I ran. He would have an audience at his full attention as he ridiculed me. I wanted to fall through the floor and never run in front of people ever again.

I remember how alienated I felt. I was, first off, the only one in the school with very large breast and developed. The mandatory gym outfit we had to wear was humiliating because the shorts were very short and would ride up the middle because I had thick thighs. I began to think there was something really wrong with me, almost like a freak of nature. I just could not understand at that time why guys made fun of me and never wanted to ask me to be a girlfriend to them like the other girls. I learned later that older guys appreciated my developed body and knew how to show how much they appreciated it, unlike guys my age.

Once I entered high school, I had come to the conclusion no guys would ever really like me, so screw it. I knew older guys paid attention to me, so I was fine. But like everything in life, certain events can bring you to your knees from excruciating pain being inflicted on your heart. That event would take place in eleventh grade and leave another lasting effect on my psyche into adulthood. That infamous event would be Valentine's Day, the most loved and hated holiday to exist.

I was sitting in class next to my buddy when a girl came in to the class with all of these roses. I looked at my buddy baffled at the fact that class could be interrupted by the "beautiful and popular" kids. So the girl went to the popular girl that was in our class and handed all of the roses to her. The look on her face was smug as she enjoyed basking in the jealous looks from everyone in the class. Of course, her followers praised and worshipped her, congratulating her gifts, an outward display of someone/someone's love and adoration for her.

All I felt was the reminder of being constantly rejected and never having someone adore me. My heart was in so much pain that I thought I was about to pass out. The pain transcended me to a dark place full of shredded pieces of glass slicing through every part of my flesh that was exposed. Then ending with extra thin slices through my heart. As bad as I wanted to cry, I just couldn't because the pain was so severe. My buddy began to talk to me and rescued me out of that nightmare place I sunken into. Later that day, my buddy gave me a rose. All I could do was choke back the tears and try to say thank you as my buddy just hugged me. I never forgot that act of kindness from my buddy.

As an adult, I had the freedom to do whatever I wanted without feeling trapped. With everything in life, actions have consequences whether good or bad. I learned how to cope with my insecurities and self-esteem with liquor. In order to face coworkers at job functions, or hanging out with friends at a party, I needed that liquid courage to face my demons. It is amazing how conversations and moments can be severely distorted with liquor making everything seem like a big happy party, not a walking disaster. I think I knew I was a walking disaster but craved the attention by any means necessary. When a valued person in my life decided to hold an intervention for me, it changed my life and forced me to deal with the battle within me.

After everything was finished, I was left with a question only I could answer. It was, "What do you want in life from this relationship?"

I just sat there and pondered on this one question, because in order to answer it meant I had to look internally at myself. It took a couple of months for me to settle my demons that tormented me in secret. The healing began by conquering the battle within me. I slowly began to love me and value my body. I noticed that men didn't think I was ugly and fat, but that I was attractive and had a beautiful, healthy body. I was only able to accept that when I accepted it from me. That whole time, my mind and tormenting demons were deceiving me. A whole world was created in my head of immediate rejection which almost destroyed me.

Love can only start within your own head. Although I realized that late in life, at least I realized it eventually. This will always be a constant battle for me to conquer, and I intend on winning each time. I will remain diligent and prepared to go toe to toe with my tormenting demons of self-esteem and self-image for the rest of my life.

The First

I was 12 when you first awakened my appetite. You had bedroom eyes, a tanned complexion, tall, slim, with evenly plumped lips, and a deep voice. Each time you spoke, the sound of your voice drew me in and placed me into a trance. I stood in front of you and you took my hand. Your gentle touch sent electric shocks throughout my body. As you gazed deep into my eyes to see my soul, you asked me to make a secret promise to you. Without any hesitation, I did.

His name was Troy. We grew up together, but he was older than me by five years. There was always a strong sexual connection between us. Therefore, I knew when I made the secret promise to him, I would be his forever. The only detail Troy had given me was that the promise would be fulfilled in four years.

It was now four years later and time for the promise to take place. Troy referred to it as "the promise ceremony." He suggested I have a special drink, since it was my first time. He said it was part of the ceremony, so I trusted his word and swallowed every gulp. Troy then escorted me down a long hallway into a dimly lit room. The king-sized bed was covered with a plush red blanket, five huge red and white pillows, and a large lamp next to the top of the bed. He walked me to the side of the bed and slowly touched me. Suddenly, my body immediately went into shock because something unfamiliar was happening to it. But once the shock started to fade away, I felt an intense aching to have more. The secret promise I made was that he would be the first man to have me. So as promised, at the age of 16, I gave my body to him.

Everything seemed to go in slow motion, allowing me to feel every sensation, fingertip, kiss, and hug before he finally took all of me. But before Troy took me, he asked a question. He said, "Have you given your body to anyone else? Or have you kept your promise and saved it for me?"

I answered him, saying, "I kept myself only for you as I promised."

As the powerful drink paralyzed my whole body, something unexpected happened. Troy had begun to transform to someone else. His form now was of a bronze color, with hazel eyes that glowed, chiseled features, perfectly shaped lips, and a gold tongue. He pretended he was Eros, the god of lust and sexual desire. As he looked deep into my eyes he captivated all of my attention. As I inhaled he inhaled my soul, allowing me to receive inside of me his nine inches by three inches of pure delight. I was transported to his world. It was a heavy fragrance of intoxicating aromas. It was the smell of lust, desire, forbidden fruits, and plain old fashioned sex! His delightful tool released his sweet nectar which transported me back to my own world. This would bind us forever he stated as he changed his form back into Troy.

Hours later, I would wake up from the promise ceremony. Dazed and confused by my surroundings, I slowly sat up, and then realized I was all alone. The only thing left in the room was the lingering smell of spilled Hennessy mixed with the odor of body fluids. I held on to the walls as I searched for the bathroom. As I entered the bathroom, looking back at me was my reflection.

Suddenly, I felt a sharp pain coming from between my legs. I dropped to my knees, closed my eyes, and remembered. I remembered being brutalized by Troy and two others. I remembered Troy possessed with hazel eyes that glowed, the other with chiseled features and bronze color, and the last one with perfectly shaped lips and a gold tongue. As Troy had brutalized my trust, soul, and body; the others could only brutalize my body. It had appeared my brain transported me to an imaginary place to protect my fragile mind from breaking during that traumatizing act.

As I sank further into the cold tiled black and white floor I disconnected from reality. I slowly succumbed to the voices that had said, "Let go." I allowed my brilliant imagination to transport me to the world I thought I went to with Troy. The world of love, desire, and pure delight; having enjoyed every moment with him as I willing gave myself to him. I would forever remain happy in this world as I slipped into darkness.

The Wish

Imagine believing like a wolf that you will be eventually found by your true soulmate. The rush of confidence and self-worth that comes along with knowing only one person can ever truly love you and will find you come hell or high water. Never doubting regardless of the amount of time that may have passed, you know you are being hunted.

I never envisioned my love life as a fairytale. In fact, I thought I would never find love nor be deserving of receiving love. It wasn't like I didn't want to be happy and live the rest of my life with someone. But in actuality, could I really find a person to truly love? Love with every ounce of life in my body? A person who could accept my imperfections that I kept secret? A person that could still find me beautiful in my ugliest acting state? A person like this does not exist in this reality, so I thought.

It was an unusually warm October evening when a small spark of magic took place. The fragrances that saturated the warm air smelled of allspice, nutmeg, cinnamon, pumpkin pie spice, and warm baked apple pie. The orange, yellow, and brown colored leaves partially stuck on the wet pavement, which was freshly coated by the fall shower. Other leaves rustled and blew down the street with the cooling wind which exposed the bareness of the trees. It was calming to say the least in the atmosphere, a reverence of some sorts. I could have never imagined a wish summonsed from my inner most being would be granted.

As the night progressed, I finally arrived to the event of the year, "The Ballroom Extravaganza." As I approached the doors in the vestibule, lined up in formation was the most breathtaking evening gowns. It looked like the Met Gala attire. I felt so underdressed even though I was just there as a spectator. As I entered through the glass doors lined with gold leaves around the borders, I walked slowly to fully ingest the beauty that was all around. I was, as usual, conscious of my behavior, so I didn't linger. I was ushered through the final doors, led down the freshly vacuumed, plush red carpet to the second aisle, middle center seat.

I sat among strangers because I attended this event alone, which had become a common practice. That week, I sat and recited love spells, so they could be manifested in the real world. I thought why couldn't I be happy and find love like everyone else? I gave in to the powers of magic that was an inherited gift that flowed through the blood lines of my family lineage. This would be my last hope at finding the love of my life or the love of my life finding me. Either way, I just knew one of us would find the other with this spell or wish and that it would take place that night.

As the lights began to dim in the theatre, a man was ushered to the vacant seat on the right side of me. As he sat down, it was like a charming spell had been blown into the air. The lights continued to be dimmed until it became total dark. In the midst of this mystical atmosphere, an intoxicating aroma had been released. The perfumed musk was light, along with warm vanilla notes, with a prolonged pear smell. It paralyzed my whole body immediately after I inhaled it. Suddenly I heard a deep, seduction, calming voice say, "Hello, do you have enough room to rest your arm? I sometimes take up both arm rests."

His voice penetrated right through, freeing my paralyzed body. As I turned to answer, I became speechless. His luminous smile, which enhanced the warmth in his eyes, his perfectly shaped full lips along with his facial hair perfectly trimmed, and his honey bronze with red undertone complexion captivated my heart. I knew this was the man I was waiting for my whole life.

As the show came to an end the lights slowly came back on, not realizing I was holding the love of my life hand during the whole performance. We enjoyed the rest of the night taking in the scenery of the bright lights on Times Square. The connection we had was unbreakable and knew it would last forever. On our finally goodbyes for the night, he leaned in slowly and kissed my cheek causing my body to become weightless and levitate in the air. He admitted to me that I was his true soulmate whom he had been hunting for his whole life. He imprinted on my heart like a wolf does when he finds his life mate. I wasn't sure if our final connection was a direct result of my reciting of magical love spells or a true divine intervention from above. I did not care at this point because I was finally happy and believed in the power of love again.

Within the Darkness

Do you remember when we first met? Well, I do, you introduced yourself to me as "Protector." In fact, you were more than just a protector, you were my friend, encourager, defender, and soulmate. From the very start, your gentle yet seducing power drew me in and captivated me. I never imagined how awakened it would make me feel to have unleashed pure fury on anyone who stood in our way. MY GOD, THE POWER WE HAD TOGETHER I LIVED FOR!

To look from the outside, it was an unhealthy merging of two souls eventually becoming one. The sadistic acts of passion became an addiction that I grew dependent on. The very thought of breaking away from our existence was absurd. Being a master craftsman, you worked my soul. Forging it like the perfect sword, a piece worthy of praise from any blacksmith. You took your time with me because you knew how much potential I had buried dormant within me. You could see the powers of darkness that was hidden, and with the right guidance could wreak havoc in the deadliest of ways.

The deadliest consequences happened after our souls became forged as one. It was such an intense power that surged through US each time we devoured the unsuspecting. I loved us together, but that would all end the night of the fight. That night, my life changed forever because "Protector" manifested into her true form.

He was special, one of kind, never to be duplicated. I made the tragic mistake of believing I could love him and separate into my own being again. "Protector" allowed me to believe I could and laid dormant in my innermost being. She also made sure no remnants of existence could be detected, so I thought. I didn't know that our souls would never be separated because we had entirely become one person. Dual personalities residing in one human body, only to be separated by death.

He told me how much he loved me as he gazed deep into my eyes. He smiled, then touched my face gently with his whole hand, kissed me softly on the lips, and then on my left cheek. He slowly positioned himself on the couch, so he could see my whole face. His expression transformed from being loved to being loathed. His eyes pierced through my heart with cold daggers. I was speechless at his change. It was as if I slipped into a nightmare! He stood up, walked towards the window, pulled back the blue and gold quilted curtains, and laughed. He turned towards me and with a sadistic demeanor said, "Do you know how much of a joke you are to me? The very idea that I would love something like you is comical! You disgust me to my core, you fat piece of UGH! You're not even WORTH the words to finish that statement! What? Are you going to cry now like the PATHETIC LOSER that you are? Ha Ha Ha Ha Ha, YOU ARE SUCH A JOKE!"

As I consumed those words, it was like I was drinking acid and feeling it burn away the insides of my stomach. My heart was beating and crying inside of my chest, taking my breath away. He placed his hand on my chest to locate exactly where my heart was beating. His hand metamorphosed into a claw, like a skilled heart surgeon, so he could rip out my heart. I was weakened from the onslaught of his words. He consumed my soul by using venomous words to weaken me so he could have absolute power.

I watched as my blood, thick as molasses and rich in wine color, dripped down my legs onto my feet. As I took in my final breath, I looked down to watch the claw pull out my heart. Suddenly, a hand emerged from my chest! I couldn't feel anything at this point because I was completely numb. The hand pushed out the claw before my heart could be removed. As the hand pushed out the claw, an arm followed, shoulder, head, and lastly a whole body. The figure that came out of me fought off my attacker, the man I loved with all of my heart. I slid down the wall and sat in my thick, molasses, wine-colored blood for comfort. I heard loud yelling, glass breaking, and then a deafening silence as I fell unconscious.

I was woken up by a very familiar smell. It was the smell that lingered whenever "Protector" appeared. "Protector," my trusted soulmate who had been with me the whole time said, "I'm Lyssa, the Greek goddess of mad rage, fury, and crazed frenzy. I was assigned from your birth to protect you. That's why I had to separate from you to protect you from the man you had loved." I faded back into unconsciousness.

As I opened up my eyes again, I was in the hospital bed. The lights were blinding, and I panicked from the tubes in my nose. The nurse ran over and grabbed my hands and comforted me. I asked, "Where am I?"

The nurse replied, "Miss, you lost a large amount of blood and was found with cuts all over your chest. The best doctor was on call tonight, so you were in excellent hands. You were in pretty bad shape, but that guy who did that to you, well, he's dead. He was a coward and jumped out the window, so he wouldn't have to answer for what he did to you. Just rest for now and the doctor will be in momentarily."

I looked around for Lyssa, but she was nowhere to be found.

I turned the faucet water on to a lukewarm temperature, catching the water in the palms of my hands. As I dried my face, I looked at my reflection in the mirror. Deep in the reflection, I saw Lyssa looking back at me!

I yelled, "WHAT ARE YOU DOING IN THE MIRROR, WHAT'S GOING ON LYSSA!"

The moment she attempted to respond, the voice that spoke back was mine. OH MY GOD! Have I imagined her the whole time? Was it me who spoke to my inner self to justify the actions I took as "Protector"? I closed my eyes tight figured I could awaken again to complete sanity. I counted to 10 low under my breath and on 10 opened up my eyes. The person who looked back at me, who took pleasure in executing rage on others, in particular the man who I loved, was me. In the mirror was not Lyssa the Greek goddess of mad rage, fury, and crazed frenzy. Lyssa was actually my alter ego who always existed deep within me. My protector, friend, encourager, defender, soulmate, and MONSTER was the real me.

CPSIA information can be obtained
at www.ICGtesting.com
Printed in the USA
LVHW082237310122
709794LV00026B/503

9 781636 612805